EMPIRICAL
EVIDENCE

EMPIRICAL EVIDENCE

16 Short Stories on God's Presence

JULIAN PHILIPS

CITI OF
BOOKS

CITIOFBOOKS, INC.
3736 Eubank NE Suite A1
Albuquerque, NM 87111-3579
www.citiofbooks.com
Hotline: 1 (877) 389-2759
Fax: 1 (505) 930-7244

Ordering Information:
Quantity sales. Special discounts are available on quantity purchases by corporations, associations, and others. For details, contact the publisher at the address above.

Printed in the United States of America.

ISBN-13:	Softcover	979-8-89391-521-1
	Hardcover	979-8-89391-522-8
	eBook	979-8-89391-523-5

Library of Congress Control Number: 2025902479

FOREWORD

I first met Julian Phillips several years ago when I was working out in the gym and noticed this sweaty man out of the corner of my eye who looked vaguely familiar working out on the cross training machine immediately next to me. He paused to begin talking to a woman who was very distraught over a situation concerning her daughter. I tried not to eavesdrop but they were right next to me when then I noticed he was openly praying for her! In the gym! When he was finished and not being one to miss out on such spiritual opportunities I immediately joined the conversation. We quickly learned that we were both serious Christians who are not shy about their faith. I realized why he looked familiar when I learned he was the Fox News anchor I would see every Saturday morning on my television. I was, apparently, a fan.

Thereafter I was privileged to run into Julian at various other times and places, besides the gym. It seemed that whenever there was some Christian event or other, even in obscure places, I would run into Julian: at a crowded rally for New York City churches, at a dinner upstate to honor an honorary doctoral degree for my former professor and other odd venues. It was all quite strange how he simply would cross my path. These chance encounters quickly grew into a solid friendship and I eventually got to know the man behind the public persona.

I also got to know this man when he was at the depths of his crisis mentioned in the book about his loss of a career path that was clearly so dear to him. He was utterly at a loss to understand how God would allow him to lose such a basic part of his identity. He was on a career trajectory that seemed unstoppable when it all came to a screeching halt, at least for a time. I cannot imagine what that would be like. I cannot imagine what it would be to not be able to practice law and represent the clients whom I love so much. This was Julian's situation shortly after I met him. He was unable to do what he most wanted to be doing. I felt his pain. Julian is indeed a talented and intelligent journalist, to which his numerous awards so well attest but he is much more than that. Julian is a man of God who loves Jesus Christ. That is what makes him special. He has a caring love for others which permeates his life. He also has an obvious anointing for personal and public ministry. It was clear to me that God was doing something in this wonderful man that only God understood, certainly not me and clearly not even Julian. While Julian states that he "lost his faith" in all reality he never lost his faith, at all. What he lost was his theology, exactly as Job did in the Bible. This happens. Julian, like Job, never lost his faith in God. They both were simply puzzled and understandably upset at what God was doing in their lives. I have been there---it hurts. It never seems good at the time but it always results in long term blessings we could never anticipate. Why? Because God loves us even more than we love ourselves and He knows what is best for us. This is true even when we cannot see it.

Empirical evidence for God often takes the form of strange events which can be explained in no other way than by God's obvious and direct involvement in or lives. Some call these 'coincidences', others call them 'miracles'. Still, others call these 'divine appointments'. Julian calls them 'empirical evidence'. Whatever you want to call these strange events they are a constant reminder that God does indeed love His children if we are only willing to let Him do it His way and trust Him and His plans for us. It may take a lifetime for such things to make sense. It may not make sense until the day we stand before God in eternity but it will make sense someday. That much is sure.

Take a journey with Julian as he undergoes a crisis of life and career along with a crisis of theology and learn that God does indeed 'work in mysterious ways'.

Dan Buttafuoco

Founding Partner
Buttafuoco & Associates

INTRODUCTION

Most often, life presents us with a seemingly endless series of challenges, tests and trials. For believers in Christ, trials are usually most difficult, because during these times our faith is tested and sometimes – even for the strongest believers, (if we are honest with ourselves), doubt can set in. Let's face it, some of God's greatest warriors had doubts. Gideon perhaps is one of the most famous examples, but there is also John the Baptist, a mighty man of God, who when in prison and facing certain death, questioned whether or not Jesus was actually the Christ. Even after numerous miracles, Jesus' own disciples at times had doubts and fears about His sovereignty. So with these examples presented to us in the Bible, how are we any different? Better yet, how are we sure that "God be with us" as is stated in the scriptures? More importantly, can we count on God to answer us, comfort us – or even give us signs that He is there when we need Him? Better yet, is there really a *personal* relationship that exists between us and the God of this universe? Through faith we certainly believe – but how does this relationship become *real* and securely rooted in our souls?

Whether we are looking to explain or defend our faith to non-believers or are just depending on God to give us direction to solve a particular problem or the very purpose for our existence, I believe the only way to know beyond a shadow of a doubt is through a personal revelation of God to an individual – or *EMPERICAL EVIDIENCE.* The dictionary defines empirical as:

Based on, concerned with, or verifiable by observation or experience rather than theory or pure logic.

In other words, no matter how many times you read in the scriptures of God's relationship with Abraham, Moses, Daniel and the prophets, the bottom line is God is not *real* unless He is *real* to YOU! We all at some point thirst and hunger for empirical evidence!

Now, if we examine the relationships God had with His people, we see examples of this empirical evidence throughout the Bible. Gideon, as I mentioned earlier needed to *know* for certain God wanted Him to lead

His people in battle, so he asked God not once, but several times to give him signs to remove his doubts, (Judges 8: 36-40); God used a burning bush that was not consumed by the flames to get the attention of Moses, (Exodus 3:2); Daniel prayed for revelation and God answered by sending His messenger Gabriel with a timely Word, (Daniel 9:23). The list goes on and on in both the Old and New Testaments and are too numerous to mention in this introduction of how God gave, by grace, empirical evidence to guide, strengthen and comfort His people. So the question remains, how do I get this empirical evidence? How does God become personal and real to me? The answer is to simply examine your life to see how God has acted on your behalf! Empirical evidence is most often not found in the grandiose or spectacular events in our lives, but rather in the simple circumstances or events that we encounter on a daily basis. Things that we may often overlook – or even take for granted.

Is God a personal God? Does He really care about you and what concerns you? The answer is yes! Through my obedience and gratefulness for the empirical evidence God has personally revealed to me, I will share 16 short stories of how God has let me know He has been with me not only in times of trial and crisis – but when He needed to use me to help change a life or reveal His power. These stories are real with no exaggeration or embellishment. I pray they provide peace and nourishment to your souls for the journey ahead!

Blessings,

Julian

TABLE OF CONTENTS

1
"FAITH DEFIES LOGIC"

Three years after leaving Fox News, I was still out of work, and no prospects in sight. The country was in the midst of a financial breakdown and the mortgage crisis was in full bloom. Millions of people were facing foreclosure and my wife Barbara and I were certainly prime candidates – not because we had a sub-prime loan, but simply because I could not 'buy' a job. The situation seemed strange to me because I co-hosted the number one weekend cable morning news show in the country for four years. I was well liked with a good reputation and no 'baggage'. To a person almost everyone thought that some station or network would pick me up immediately, however, not one bite - zilch! Years of prayer and trusting God seemed to yield nothing and I was starting to lose faith.

A good friend of mine, Mark Lacher, President of the Koeppel Auto group, presides over a number of car dealerships under the Koeppel umbrella. Mark and I have been friends for many years and he is a generous man with a warm heart. Knowing my situation, he offered me a job as a service manager. Now I guess pride got in the way – no, let me take that back. Pride DID get in the way! I just could not see myself going from an Emmy award winning news anchor, to a uniform wearing service manager for a Nissan dealership in Jackson Heights, Queens! Now pride has a funny way of taking a back seat to the reality of making mortgage payments and paying bills. I had to do something, so instead of facing the embarrassment of someone in the dealership recognizing me taking orders for parts and service on their cars in a crowded dealership, I decided to take an 'undercover' job for Mark, and that was riding 'clunker' cars from his Nissan dealership in Queens to an auction house 60 miles away in central New Jersey. This in exchange for newer cars from the auction house back to the dealership. The salary? $25 dollars per car! It was a grueling ordeal. Driving a 'clunker' from the dealership to the auction house and back with the newer car to Mark's used car lots. A 120 mile round-trip excursion. I would get up around 5 o'clock and get to the dealership around 5:45am before the rush hour kicked in. Then the ordeal of trying to make that round trip with as many cars as I could. For about a week I managed to make about $75 dollars a day. Time and traffic – not to mention fatigue, took its toll. Mark being the stand-up guy he is, upped the price to $50 per car, but both he and I knew this was not going to pay the bills. Once again, Mark offered the service job, but there was a catch! Mark said he was not willing to take the time or money to train me for this job if I was not willing to agree to seriously consider making a career change and forgetting about going back into the news biz. Now that was fair on Mark's part, however it was a deal breaker for me – and at the same time a sense of relief. Give up news? Suppose I took that job and all of a sudden a network called offering me a news or reporting gig? The temptation to once again do what I *knew* God had gifted me to do was too great to turn my back on it to take car part orders! Was this a leap of faith, or just a foolish move in order to save my pride? Pride or not, I decided to keep my options open and hope a news gig would surface.

About a month later I was still on the skids. No prospects for a job, any job, and after walking with the Lord for nearly 15 years I decided to throw in the towel. I lost my faith! That morning I had a doctor's appointment and I took the 7:36am Long Island Railroad train into Penn Station for a 9:30 date with the doctor. My wife Barbara was also taking the same train to work. On the way to the train station I told Barbara that I had lost faith. This was not a good move. Barbara was not only surprised but greatly troubled by this news and she made no bones about expressing her concern. Needless to say, a normally talkative ride into Penn Station was quiet. Not much said, nevertheless I was not backing down. I was done! I truly believed God had abandoned me, or at the very least was not listening to my prayers. Had I done something wrong? I was tired of trying to figure it out. The only scripture I could think of was one I had held on to for years in the book of Psalms:

"I was young and now am old, and I have never seen the righteous forsaken or their children begging bread". Psalm 37:25

Well that may have been the case for David who wrote it, but what about me? I needed *empirical evidence!*

Dr. David Kamlet is a gifted internist and a good friend. We are the same age, and for more than 20 years I have trusted David with my medical needs. During most visits I'm sure other patients would get annoyed because before, during and after my exams we would spend a considerable amount of time talking politics and world affairs, not to mention things of a personal nature. Putting two highly opinionated people together in a room perhaps is not always the best thing, but I was always amazed at how much knowledge David could share on almost any topic. We have a bond and the conversation would automatically flow as soon as he entered the examination room! But this time would be different. No talk on my part on politics or personal matters – I just wanted an exam and then take the next train east headed home.

"How's it going Julian?" David asked with a grin, waiting for a hug. "Fine", I said with a deadpan face and no willingness to embrace my dear friend. Dead silence for what seemed like an eternity.

"Faith defies logic you know, Julian", David said while he was checking my blood pressure. "Excuse me?" I said. "Faith defies logic you know". He said again.

Where was this coming from? I did not mention anything about faith to him, or my lack of it at the time. David is Jewish and he went on to talk about how Moses parted the Red Sea after leading the Israelites out of Egypt. After the exam and back in his office, he took out some old book written in Hebrew and mentioned something about how the Red Sea did not actually part until one Israelite, who he named from this strange little book of his, took a leap of faith and jumped into the water. At that point, I knew there was something, or *someone* involved in this conversation and I humbled myself to listen to more. David then started talking about how Winston Churchill, (one of my favorite statesmen), became one of the youngest leaders ever elected to the British Parliament, but how after a short while was forgotten about and for nearly a decade or more had fallen into relative obscurity.

"But then World War Two came on the horizon, threatening the world and the British Empire. Churchill was the right leader for that tumultuous time in history. He was needed again. There will be a time when you will be needed again too, Julian."

Three months later, I went back to David's office for a follow-up visit. Still intrigued, I brought up that conversation we had during the last visit. He did not remember it. Very unusual for a man that remembers just about everything. In case you might think Barbara called David before I got to his office, she does not have his number. Besides, it would not dawn on her to call David on a personal or spiritual matter. She did tell me however she called our pastor, as soon as she got to work to tell him of my dilemma. She never heard back from him. I'm certain God wanted to take care of this matter *personally*.

2

"SMALL CHANGE"

Four years into our financial wilderness, Barbara and I were still, by some miracle, able to hold on to our house. We were fortunate enough to get a loan modification, which certainly helped – not to mention, aid from our church, the Christian Cultural Center and our beloved Pastor, Dr. A.R. Bernard. The church has a broadcast ministry and I was asked to produce some news stories for the church, plus perform some public relations duties for Pastor Bernard. This, combined with Barbara's part-time job in the Development office at Northside Center for Child Development in Harlem and her gigs singing jazz in some of the top clubs in New York and around the country kept us afloat. It was certainly a blessing, however I had used up all of my stellar credit to pay the bills and the mortgage. Needless to say after working for years in the broadcast industry and making good money, I had enough of a nest egg to pay the mortgage for a few years. The law of supply and demand, however, is no respecter of man, and after a long period of no full-time work, the lack of supply of money simply could not keep up with the demand of the bills coming in. At last, I had finally used up all of my credit on both credit cards and prayed for something do develop on the job front.

Lo and behold, I got a call from Bill Thompson, the New City Comptroller. I've known Bill for quite some time. I consider him a friend and we have spent some time over the years playing golf together. Bill was kind enough to give me a part time job in his Press Office. Now it was not enough to pay all the bills – but it took some of the weight off of our shoulders. Every day, Barbara and I would catch the same train together and venture into the city. She would head uptown, and I would go downtown to the Municipal building that housed the offices of the City Comptroller. One February morning as we were both leaving the house, I told Barbara that I was down to my last twenty three dollars. This was all I had left after depleting my savings and credit accounts. I was waiting for a check from the City Comptrollers' office, which would not come for another week. I would have to depend on Barbara during that period for food and transportation just to get to work.

"I have twenty three dollars in the bank, just enough to get some lunch and take the peak train back home" I said to Barbara on the way to the train that morning. "Ok," she said. "We'll find a way to make it until your check comes" Barbara said in a reassuring voice. I'll tell you, trials and challenges have a way of letting you know just who really has your 'back' and the people who are really important to you. Barbara was and is my soul mate and truly was tested in the 'crucible of crises'. What a God send!

At lunch time, I left the fifth floor of the Municipal building and ventured out into the cold to make my way through City Hall Park to the CitiBank across the street. There, I would withdraw my remaining funds. After inserting my card into the ATM machine and punching in my I.D. number, the monitor revealed 'no available funds'. No available funds?! Somehow I must have miscalculated my account balance. I tried again. 'No available funds'. I did have an account at Capital One, but that dried up a few months back.

With only two dollars and change to my name left in my pocket, I left the bank and was immediately hit by a mixture of snow and rain. As I walked passed City Hall Park back to work, I began to think of my parents. Both had long passed, but I remembered if I ever needed anything, they would always be there. Now they weren't and suddenly I started to fell all alone. Loneliness can be pretty overwhelming. I started to cry.

"All the Emmy's I've won and all the other awards I've received over the years and I've been reduced to this. I have nothing to show for it!" I cried out to the Lord. "I don't even have enough money to get back home. If you are who you say you are, I want you to get me enough money to catch the off-peak train home. I can ask somebody at work to give be some small change to make up the difference with what I have, but I'm not going to ask a soul! I want you to give me the money!" I composed myself in time and dried up the tears before I got to the Municipal building. After getting off on the fifth floor. I made it to the cubby hole where I worked and proceeded to take off my coat. As I was about to hang it up on the coat tree, I heard a jingling of coins in the outer pocket. I reached in. There were several coins, and some dollars bills. Enough not only to get on the off-peak train back home – but a little left over to buy a paper, or whatever else I might have wanted!

It was the coldest day of the year. It was the first time I wore that particular coat all winter. Had I not put on that coat…Coincidence – or empirical evidence?

3

"Spiral Cut Ham"

It's absolutely amazing the things we take for granted in life, and how some of the simplest pleasures take on a new meaning, when you don't have them anymore. Take for instance a spiral cut honey glazed ham. Now for as long as I can remember, we would always have a spiral cut honey glazed ham at Christmas for my mother-in-law, Thelma King. It was a no brainer! But this Christmas was different. Barbara and I simply could not afford one. Things were that tight.

"I really wish we could afford to get the ham for mom", I said to Barbara one day in the living room. "It just doesn't seem like Christmas without one".

A few days later, our real estate broker and long-time friend Ginny Pergola called on the phone.

"Are you guys going to be home for a while?" she said. "I'm in the neighborhood, and I wanted to stop by and say hello."

"Sure thing," we said.

A few minutes later, Ginny comes in the front door with a small package of her cookies she bakes and gives out to friends and family every year – but she also had this big package with her.

"I've never done this before," she exclaimed, "but something told me you two might like a spiral cut honey glazed ham for Christmas."

There was a long moment of silence. *Something?*

Every year since then, Ginny has given us a spiral cut honey glazed ham for Christmas.

4

"A Seed Toward Greatness"

For four years, Friday night was a special time for my college roommate and I. At the stroke of midnight, you could count on the fact that we both would be on the top steps of the Executive Building on the campus of Purdue University with our old reliable friend – a bottle of Boone's Farm Apple wine. Byron was from East Orange, New Jersey and I was from Queens, New York. The seventies was a very interesting time socially for two young black men from the east coast, attending a socially conservative school in the heart of the midwest. Needless to say there were many times we both wondered why we came so far to go to college to get an education. The antidote to all of our frustrations was that bottle we shared on the steps of the Executive Building every Friday at midnight. It just seemed to ease some of the pain as we talked about what life would be like after we graduated and moved on with our lives.

Thirty years later on a warm Friday night in 2007, I found myself on top of the steps of the Executive Building at the stroke of midnight. This time without Byron, or that bottle of Boone's Farm. Byron was a successful engineer and I was a year out of work from Fox News. A few months before, I was asked to deliver the keynote address to professors and students attending the Big Ten Diversity Conference on campus. This was a huge deal as more than one thousand academics from the Big Ten Conference and other colleges and universities around the country gathered to discuss issues of inclusion and diversity. Sally Mason, a good friend, was the Provost at Purdue, and former President of the University of Iowa.

"I would be honored if you would accept my offer to be our keynote speaker," said Sally. "Well alright", I said somewhat reluctantly. How could I turn Sally down? We created a bond over the years, and talked about many issues facing Purdue, which I believe was a much more progressive University under her leadership. The problem was, I had been unemployed for a year. Feeling down on my luck, what advice could I give these educators and students? Keep hope alive? Hardly the case when I felt I didn't have much hope for myself at the time.

I sat there on those steps, listening to the sounds of West Lafayette, Indiana. Thirty years has a way of changing things. An already large campus was much larger. The midnight silence was now replaced by the sounds of cars and trucks and the usual shouts of partying students, who perhaps had too much to drink, either on their way home or going to another party.

"Just what do you want me to tell these people Lord?" I cried out. "I have nothing to share at this point. My career is on hold and I would be a hypocrite to share a message of hope when I'm not feeling it right now." The night before a major speech and I had nothing concrete to talk about.

Gary Anglin was the Praise and Worship leader for the Christian Cultural Center. He was also a Chaplain and spent a lot of time visiting the sick and shut-in at hospitals, not to mention singing at various venues all over the tri-state area. He was the real deal, a man who lived by the scriptures and was living testimony to the power of the Word of God. Gary had overcome many physical challenges and illnesses. Oddly enough, Gary looked much younger than his years and seemed stronger than ever as the years passed. Somehow my thoughts turned to him and the time he told me when he had to deliver a speech in Jamaica, West Indies.

"The man who spoke before me was very good Julian and I still did not know how I could follow such a strong and powerful message."

"What did you do?" I asked.

"The Lord told me to give them my testimony" he said. Needless to say, Gary's remarks were very well received.

"That's it! I'll give them my testimony!" I said to myself. I jumped up off the steps and immediately walked across campus to the Purdue Memorial Union to rest up and prepare for the keynote address later that evening.

The crowd was much bigger than even I expected and far noisier than I anticipated. When Sally introduced me, I made my way to the podium and looked over a sea of people who I was not sure how they would accept what I was about to say. I talked about trials and challenges that many would face on their journey after college. How it would not all be easy at times. I stressed the importance of faith and perseverance and wove in stories of my life and where I was at that very moment – unemployed. Well, I got a standing ovation. Quite relieved after delivering the address, and believing I had done God's work, there was no doubt in my mind that God would now *deliver* me from unemployment and place me back into the world of network news.

Four months later, I found myself walking down a corridor of the City Comptrollers' office. I was making my way to the bathroom and I could not escape the fact that I felt depressed that I still was not back in the 'big leagues' and could only find part-time work.

For some reason, I reached into my suit jacket pocket and felt a piece of paper. Pulling it out, I realized it was a check written out to me. The date on the check was July 28th – the same day I delivered the keynote address at Purdue! It was in the amount of fifty dollars from a women from Illinois. The amount was not as significant as what was written by her on that line in the lower left-hand corner saying what the check was for. 'A Seed Toward Greatness' is what she wrote. The funny thing is I don't remember the woman, or her giving me the check. Furthermore, I've worn that suit many times since the July presentation and never felt it in my suit jacket pocket until November 28th, four months to the day it was *given* to me.

The 28th has always been a special day of any month ever since then. My website is titled as 'A Seed Toward Greatness'. I now have a Ministry which was incorporated in the state of New York in 2013. It is called 'A Seed Toward Greatness'.

5

"A WALK WITH GOD"

On the morning of October 4th 1997, I woke up early and eager to attend a prayer rally on the National Mall in Washington, D.C. I spent the night at my close friend Henry Osborne's home in Silver Spring, Maryland in anticipation for what I was expecting to be a momentous experience in the presence of God with thousands of other Christian men.

It was a day rally of prayer and speakers entitled 'Stand in the Gap', sponsored by Promise Keepers an organization of Christian men whose goal was to unify and strengthen Christian men in the faith. It was expected that men from around the country, and world, would make their way to the nation's capital to fellowship and experience the presence of God in a very unique and profound way.

1997 was a very pivotal year for me in many ways. My mother passed away the year before, which changed my life. She was my rock and best friend. Caring for her during a year plus battle with a rare form of cancer had taken all the strength I could muster. I can't recall all the churches and prayer meetings I attended looking for a word that might heal my mother. Countless nights, I spent on my knees in prayer crying out to God for a miracle healing. I even put together a celebrity bartending event with all of my TV and radio news colleagues to raise money for the

Carcinoid Tumor Foundation at one of my favorite local Brooklyn bars. A little more than a year later, I could still feel the pain of her loss. There was also another very important matter. It was going on two years that my wife Barbara and I were separated. Needless to say, I was looking for a word – something from God to keep me going. Anything that could bolster my faith, a shot of assurance that things would be alright I and would finally emerge from what I felt was a nightmare.

At the time, my pastor Dr. A.R. Bernard was very much involved with Promise Keepers and was one of the featured speakers. Many men from my church at Christian Cultural Center promised to make the trip and of course there were several bus loads that made the 225 mile trip down Interstate 95 from New York to Washington D. C. for the occasion.

There was no doubt in my mind I would make this trip – and there was no doubt in my mind that I would stay at Henry's house the night before. Now, those close to Henry call him the 'consummate host'. I first met Henry when I was working for WNBC-TV as their Community Relations Manager. NBC's Owned and Operated Stations would have annual retreats for their executives and within that group, the Community Relations department heads from that division had their retreats as well. I met Henry at my first retreat in Albuquerque, New Mexico.

Henry was a big man in both size and character. He is the oldest of thirteen children, a high school dropout from the south side of Chicago and Vietnam War veteran. Henry later went on to get his G.E.D. and then proceeded to get a Bachelors' degree from Brandies University and a Law Degree from George Washington University. To say he was a self-made man is an understatement. Because of his life challenges, Henry could at times become confrontational in both his personal and professional life – however he possessed a big heart and as a result people were attracted to him. I can't recall all of the social gatherings and wonderful memories at the 'Osborne compound'. It became the place to be. My relationship with Henry grew and he remains a close confidant. We shared our innermost thoughts and throughout my mother's illness and the separation between my wife and I, Henry was a sounding board and a constant source of strength and comfort.

October 4th 1997 turned out to be a very warm and sunny Saturday and my mind was on getting down to the National Mall as early as possible. I had no idea where the buses from the Christian Cultural Center would park, or if I would even be able to meet up with anyone from my church. Officials were predicting hundreds of thousands of men to descend upon the Mall. I wasn't even sure if I would be able to get close to the staging area, but I knew there would be monitors all over the place so I was content to watch all the speakers, including my pastor, from a distance if need be. The bigger question was how I was going to get there. Henry had other plans, so I was on my own. A cab was out of the question. There would be no way to make it close to the mall with all the people expected. I decided to walk to the Metro station a few miles from Henry's in downtown Silver Spring to the National Mall.

I can't explain why or how, but as I neared the Metro station *something* told me to just keep walking. I did. 10 miles all the way to the National Mall. I just started talking to God, but did not get anything I could think of in return. "Some walk with God", I said to myself. "I'm doing all the talking and I'm not hearing anything back from you!" I was getting tired and the trek down 16th Street N.W. was starting to take its' toll. "Where are you Lord?" I asked. "Can you at least give me some idea I am getting close to the rally?" I went on, not really expecting a reply at that point.

Right after I uttered those words, I slipped on the remnants of a fried chicken wing on the sidewalk and almost lost my balance. It knew it was God telling me I was close. You see, the further along 16th Street, the more fast food joints started popping up and the closer I was getting to downtown and the National Mall. "You certainly have a sense of humor don't you!" I barked back. It was the first time I realized He was actually listening to me – and the first time I got a response!

As if on cue, the National Mall was directly in front of me. At that point I became a little overwhelmed because of the enormity of the crowd. There was never any official estimate, but the number of men have been calculated to be anywhere from two hundred thousand to a million.

During the course of the day, men were listening to speakers, singing and lying face down in large numbers in prayer. There were so many people in attendance; I started to feel like a grain of sand in a five pound paper bag! If only I could get to Pastor Bernard and the men from my church, I would feel much better, and more connected.

"Can you guide me to them?" I asked God. I must admit I thought it would be an impossible task. They could have been anywhere. I decided to just keep walking through the massive crowd toward the staging area and perhaps by faith I would run into someone I knew.

It was near mid-day and it was hot for October, even in the nation's capital. After about an hour of working my way through the crowd, I saw a group of men tending to another man sitting on a bench who was suffering from the heat. That man turned out to be Elder William Pointer, who was having a hard time dealing with the heat, and some of the men from my church. The odds of finding anyone from home was slim, so I figured God, once again, had orchestrated my footsteps. About an hour later we all made our way to the stage. I remained outside while those in my group who had backstage passes went inside the staging area to hear Pastor. Not to my surprise, Pastor Bernard gave a moving speech on reconciliation. Shortly thereafter I made my way to the stage entrance – and as if on cue the gate opened and there was Pastor with a smile on his face. I gave him a big hug. It was at that point that I believe our relationship solidified.

It all started with a walk and a conversation. A conversation that was evidence that when I talked, he not only listened, but provided answers.

6

"THE VISION"

There are eight thousand, eight hundred and ten promises in the Bible. Promises of all kinds and the majority are found in the Old Testament. There are promises of health, deliverance, peace of mind, you name it. If you are in need of something, anything, you can find a promise from God if you take the time to search the scriptures.

Now God will most often not put a promise in your hand, but rather in your reach. Such was the case with my marriage to Barbara. God's promise did not come from scripture, it came from a vision. He works that way sometimes. God uses people and circumstances to give a person in need a word of comfort or guidance – even discipline! In the Bible He even used animals to get people's attention!

It had been a little more than a year into our separation, and I believed God would somehow salvage our relationship. The belief came about by my faith in His word, and a little reassurance from my pastor. Dr. Bernard sees things sometimes and I *wanted* to believe in reconciliation. The belief was not satisfied, however, until one night when I stayed up until the wee hours of the morning singing and praying to God. Now, I can't explain all the praise because my life was far from where I had envisioned it to be at that time. Barbara was gone, my mother had passed and I was in a job that I was not all that crazy about. Nevertheless, I stayed up in bed and sang and prayed until I fell asleep. It's very important for whoever reads this chapter to get this one point above anything else. *I was not singing and praying about my problems or asking anything of God. I was worshipping Him!* Worshipping Him *in spite* of my circumstances and all that I was going through.

After about an hour or so, I fell into a deep sleep. During this time I had a vision of Barbara stopping by to visit me at our home in Brooklyn. I opened the front door and there she was looking somewhat the same, but her hair was straight as an arrow without any curls. I invited her in and we had such a great time together, talking and laughing about all sorts of things. After a while I woke up and felt this incredible peace that I have never really felt before.

"That's the peace of God!" pastor Bernard exclaimed when I told him of the vision. Well it certainly seemed like it was, so I put my faith in that vision, and God's promise to me from that point on. But there was a big problem. Let me take that back, there was a huge fly in the ointment! A few months after receiving this promise, Barbara called me at work. I could tell where this conversation was headed and she finally said she wanted a divorce. A divorce! What about this promise?

The United Nations is not far from where I worked and I routinely went there during breaks to pray in their park on a bench overlooking the East River. This time I was deeply troubled and as the tears flowed down my cheeks I cried out to God. "You have made a fool out of me to all my friends! I believed your promise and told many people about this vision. Now people are laughing at me!" I went on and on trying to get some type of answer from God. After a while a seagull landed on the wooden rail directly in front of me and started making all this noise while flapping its wings! The seagulls' presence and all the racket it was making startled me. The thing is, the seagull did not stop making all the noise until I opened up my Bible I took with me and started to read. I can't explain it, but I flipped open the Bible to the book of Isaiah, chapter 43. It is entitled 'Israel's only Savior'. The whole chapter is very encouraging, but it reads in part:

"… When you pass through the waters, I will be with you; and when you pass through the rivers, they will not sweep over you. When you walk through

the fire, you will not be burned; the flames will not set you ablaze. For I am the Lord your God, the Holy One of Israel your Savior".

Well I did not move until after I finished reading that chapter. The seagull then flew away. Afterwards I actually felt a sense of peace. A year and a half later Barbara did come back. We renewed our vows and moved to Long Island. The funny thing is, when Barbara came back, her hair was styled in the exact same manner as I saw her in the vision.

7

"THE PROPHESY"

It was November 2007 and the South was hit hard by a severe drought. Georgia, Alabama and Florida were particularly hard hit. Lakes and rivers fell to record lows. Water restrictions put in place months before were not nearly enough to conserve resources.

"I'm here today to appeal to you and to all Georgians and all people who believe in the power of prayer to ask God to shower our state, our region, our nation with the blessings of water", Governor Sonny Perdue shouted to hundreds gathered outside the state capitol for a day of prayer.

Nearly a thousand miles north, I listened to the appeal on television. In a few days I along with Barbara planned to head down to Greensboro, Georgia to officiate over 'The Lighting of the Lodge' at Reynolds Plantation. Reynolds Plantation was listed as one of the best golf resorts in the world. Sitting between Atlanta and Augusta, home of the renowned Masters Tournament, Reynolds sat on thirteen thousand acres of pine forests and rolling hills on Lake Oconee. The owners were the Reynolds family, who have owned the land there for generations. We became close friends a few years back after a family member who was a big fan of my weekend morning show on the Fox News Channel, invited me down to the Masters.

Jamie Reynolds assumed responsibility for most of the operations at Reynolds. He is a tall man with a big heart, and very unassuming. In fact you might never know he was the CEO. The Ritz Carlton Lodge sits on the property. It was not uncommon to see Jamie walking through the huge lobby in wrinkled jeans, sandals and three days growth of beard on his face past high priced patrons. "I just want to be a good steward of the land", Jamie said one day as we were heading to witness a round of golf at the Masters. A good steward he was, but nature was devastating the land and Lake Oconee was shriveling up to the point of seemingly no return. Boats were pulled from their docks and you could literally walk twenty to thirty yards onto the lake were water once covered the rocky ground.

The Lighting of the Lodge was a big deal for the town of Greensboro and the surrounding communities. Literally thousands of people would come and see the Christmas lights turned on at the Ritz Carlton Lodge and the live sheep, camels and other animals that were brought in for the Manger display where actors portrayed Mary Joseph and the baby Jesus. It was a great evening of food, fun, church choirs, raffles and live auctions for charities which culminated in Santa arriving followed by a spectacular fireworks display. For the past couple of years I was honored by the Reynolds to serve as the emcee. Barbara would sing a jazzy versions of familiar Christmas songs to delight the crowd, so it always a great time, and a wonderful way to spend Thanksgiving and the beginning of the Christmas season with our friends from the south.

I arose early in the morning on the day of the lodge lighting to get up and pray. Leaving the bedroom, where Barbara was sound asleep, I ventured out into the living room of our suite at the Ritz Carlton and knelt down in front of the sliding glass doors overlooking Lake Oconee. The sun had not risen and I had been in prayer for approximately 15-20 minutes. As I was about to get up, I was forced not to my knees, but to the floor where I lay face down. I can't explain this force, but it was gentle, nonetheless powerful enough to keep me on my face for a period until I heard this voice in my head which said "It's not going to be like this always." Now I'm thinking God was telling me the drought of unemployment was about to end and I was overjoyed at the thought of finally getting back to work after leaving Fox News a year ago. However as the day drew closer to my duties as emcee for the lodge lighting later that evening, my thoughts focused on the drought that plagued Georgia and other parts of the South. I kept getting this feeling to tell the crowd that night that the drought would soon end. To be honest, weather forecaster did predict a small amount of rain the next day. Was I basing this feeling on that or was God actually speaking to me to give a prophetic word to the crowd that evening? I was not sure but the feeling kept nagging at me all day.

Right before I was set to take the stage, a few sprinkles came out of the sky, but did not last very long. No matter how bad the folks of Georgia needed that rain, I don't think anyone wanted water to spoil the festivities for that evening – not to mention myself, for in a very human, and selfish, way I now wanted to speak this prophesy of rain I felt God had given me. "What an idiot you are Julian?", I said to myself. "You just want to grandstand in front of all these people with some message in order to make yourself look like some kind of prophet." I've got to tell you, I did start to feel a little foolish and ashamed of my human frailties with this wish to feel like some man of God. But the sprinkles did stop, the show went on and the feeling to predict and end to the drought remained.

Of course, Barbara tore down the house with her great voice and it was at this moment that I got up before five thousand people to deliver 'the prophesy'. "I am here to tell you that the Spirit of God came to me early this morning and He said this drought is over!" Well the crowd was overjoyed to hear the news. I felt kind of empty after uttering those words and leaving the stage because I really was not sure if God was actually using me, or if my need to feel important took center stage.

The next morning I went out for a round of golf. I played solo, which is something I like to do especially when I want to think and reflect on things. After about the fifth hole, I started to recall the events of the night before, and my 'prophetic' words. "Lord I think I just made a terrible fool out of myself. Please forgive me if I misrepresented you. I thought you were speaking to me, but maybe I was wrong", I said while I drove the cart to the next hole. "If at all possible, don't make a fool out of me publicly. These people desperately need the rain. Let it come today", I cried out.

By this time I was on the twelfth hole, when a few drops of rain came out of the sky. "Lord, I don't know if you are answering my prayer, but could you please hold off the rain until I finish my round?" I could not believe I had the nerve to ask God for such a request. Well the request was denied. The skies opened up and within minutes there were puddles and little rivers of water making their way past the fairways and greens and into Lake Oconee. A little disappointed I could not finish the round of golf, inwardly I was beginning to really believe God spoke to me the morning before and I started to feel a sense of joy, so I let out a few shouts in the golf cart on the way back to the pro shop.

Within two weeks after steady rain, the water levels started to once again rise on the banks of Lake Oconee. The drought came to an end.

8

"AT THE 11TH HOUR"

It was nothing short of a miracle that foreclosure was not a reality much earlier during the time I was unemployed. Somehow, some way we were able to pay our bills. Generous tax returns, odd jobs, help from the church crisis fund, and of course generous friends always made up the difference. However, there comes a time when the sources dry up and the well runs dry!

Barbara and I were sitting in the living room one late afternoon watching TV. There was a knock at the door and I got up to answer it. "Are you Julian Phillips the owner of this house?" a man in his thirties dressed casually said holding a small package in his hand. "I am" I said somewhat puzzled by his presence, but I sensed this was not going to be good. "Well I'm here to serve you with this legal notice of foreclosure and you will be required to appear in court to answer this notice within 30 days. By the way good luck", he said with a very sincere look on his face as he walked away.

Foreclosures were happening everywhere across the country. Whether it was the result of sub-prime loans or the fact that more and more people were losing their jobs, millions of people were in danger of facing eviction and in extreme cases, becoming homeless. For the Phillips household, it had finally come down to this. No job prospects and now the possibility of losing our home.

We hired a lawyer, who immediately went into action and filed what is called a forbearance, which in essence 'calls off the dogs' and gives homeowners a few months before the actual eviction process starts.

"This will give me enough time to find work" I said to Barbara. Even after four years of unemployment, I had enough hope, and faith, to believe God would not let us down. Even so, the human side of me kicked in. Days and weeks after the notice of foreclosure was delivered to our front door, I was starting to mentally divorce myself from the house we lived in. I dreaded coming home on many days. I often thought about the embarrassment that I would feel when our neighbors would find out. Now, once a court order is delivered, it becomes public notice and then the vultures start to circle overhead. Barbara and I got notices in the mail on a daily basis from all sorts of lawyers and legal firms specializing in foreclosure. There were also notices from agencies offering us help through this process. To make matters worse, calls came almost daily from creditors looking to be paid. When the phone rang, we looked at the caller i.d. to see who it was from. If it was an unrecognized number, we just did not answer. Most often we knew by the number it was a creditor and did not pick up.

Months of this daily activity can either make you stronger or break you. We wanted to keep our house. It was a home and we had few choices. Sell and move back to the city, which we did not want to do, and even if we did, I would still need a job to pay a smaller mortgage or rent. The last alternative was to move into Barbara's mother brownstone in Brooklyn. Now I loved my mother-in-law, but to move in with her meant complete failure in my mind, so I fought to keep that thought at bay.

It's a tough thing not knowing what the next day will bring and I must say I had to fight the spirit of fear second-by-second on many days. We were literally two weeks away from going into foreclosure, when by chance I got a phone call that changed our fortunes.

"Hey Julian, I'm putting together another golf outing and would like to know if you would be kind enough to join my golf committee." It was Congressman Ed Towns, whom I've known over the years. "We're having a breakfast meeting at the Brooklyn Diner in the Heights. I hope you can make it". "Sure" I said, not really wanting to attend, but I had nothing else on my agenda, and the Congressman seemed like he could really use my help. I gained somewhat of a reputation over the years putting together celebrity golf outings to raise money for my church. The thing is, I was not much in the mood to reach out and help anybody at this point. Nonetheless it was a free breakfast.

The breakfast meeting was set for a week after the Congressman's call. I got to the diner early and chatted with a few other early arrivals. The meeting in and of itself was predictable. The basic role of a committee member is to find golfers who are willing to pay more than they would normally pay for a round of golf to help a cause. This time it was a political fundraiser and those can be a little harder to do, because 'politics' are involved. There is an old saying that there are no permanent friends or enemies in politics and that is so true. You just never know who is going to 'sign on' and support a politician.

Shortly after the meeting I was on my way out the front door, when Congressman Towns stopped me. "What are you up to these days Julian? I don't see you on TV anymore", he asked with a puzzled look on his face. Now I really did not want to tell him what dire straits Barbara and I were in, but I knew the Congressman pretty well, so I told him I had been unemployed for quite some time. I did not, however, mention we were facing foreclosure and I did not think he could be of any help.

"Well you can come work for me", he said and then turning to his Chief of Staff the Congressman went on, "I want to hire Julian as my Communications Director and I want you to offer him a salary that is attractive".

Within two weeks my career working in the Congressman's Brooklyn district and on Capitol Hill began. Even better, His son Daryl was an Assemblyman in Brooklyn, who just happened to serve as the Chairman of the State Banking Committee. He helped resolve our foreclosure nightmare. All of this came 'At the 11th hour'.

9

"A Prayer for Ron"

Working as a national television news anchor and host affords one the opportunity to meet a whole lot of people. The funny thing is most of the people who correspond with you around the country and world you never really meet in person. I have folk who I have communicated with by e-mail or on Facebook, but I have never met. Most of those people kind of fall by the wayside. Especially when you are no longer 'the flavor of the day'. After being off the air for five years most TV personalities are nothing but a distant memory, or like we say in golf, 'yesterday's round'.

Ron Grant was not one of those people. For whatever reason Ron sent me an e-mail at work – and I can't remember what the subject matter was. Nevertheless, I responded and we have kept in contact ever since. He was much more conservative in his political beliefs than I was. I would say Ron perhaps is more in line with the typical Fox viewer, who I was at constant odds with most of the time in my commentary during my years on Fox & Friends. For some reason, we 'clicked' and I enjoyed hearing from Ron over the years.

Ron managed a small airport in the suburbs of Philadelphia. Hs life seemed to be moving along quite well until one day I got an e-mail from him that he needed to find another job. I could sense the urgency in that e-mail and I had his number and decided to call him up.

It was mid-winter as I recall it and I was in the car taking Barbara up to a gig she had that night singing with her quartet at the legendary Lenox Lounge in Harlem. It was a cold snowy night and I'm trying to navigate the city streets while talking to Ron on the phone. Ron needed a job and he needed one fast. One thing led to another and the conversation lasted much longer than I realized. We arrived at the front of Lenox Lounge and Barbara jumped out to get inside the club and out of the cold to rehearse with the band before the first set. "I'll see you inside shortly", I promised.

About forty-five minutes later, I rushed in to take my seat before the first set started. "Where have you been? We're about to start"! Barbara jaws were tight. I have a tendency to be long winded at times and she was expecting me to be front and center. I am her biggest fan after all! "Sorry Boo, but I was praying for Ron. He's going through some things right now and I had to do the right thing by him. Barbara realized it too. It turned out to be a great night. When Barbara sings, it is always a great night.

I can't tell you how many weeks or months' time passed by, but I got one of those e-mails from Ron just to catch up on things. This is what was said in the exchange:

------Original Message------
From: Ron Grant
To: julesmp1@msn.com
Sent: Jun 28, 2011 2:38 PM
Subject: Update

How is my dear friend doing? I haven't heard
from you in a while Julian Just checking in to
say Hi
Ron Grant

From: Julian Phillips [mailto:julesmp1@msn.com]
Sent: Wednesday, June 29, 2011 7:34 AM
To: Ron Grant
Subject: Re: Update

Good morning Ron!
Really great hearing from you.
On vacation as of today. Barbara and I are going
to enjoy the Fourth out in the Hamptons (nice to
have rich friends)--and we both are expecting
new doors that have been placed before us to
reveal opportunities to us that will bring us
a financial windfall--and ways to service God's
people. How's things with you? We should talk
by phone soon.

Best,
Julian

------Original Message------
From: Ron Grant
To: julesmp1@msn.com
Sent: Jun 29, 2011 9:53 AM
Subject: RE: Update

Julian,

I feel the same way, I have rich friends too,
Rich in Faith. I am working... An aerospace
company I consulted for in Fredericksburg, VA
offered me a job quite a few months ago, however
with my 14 year old autistic son, (Michael) it's
very difficult to move him from a very successful
"public" program here in NJ to an unknown.
Unfortunately, I couldn't accept the position.
I have had to refuse a great deal of good

positions over the past two years for the very same reasons.

It's sad to see the levels of education and how much they vary throughout the US, not even considering the lack of special education programs. And unfortunately, it all equates to the income levels and educational levels of the parents in those areas. It is a vicious cycle that would make anyone give up, or give in to the system. And in my opinion some politicians do nothing to cure the problem, rather they exploit and cultivate it. I call it the "vote farm".

Anyway back to the consulting job in VA, a month later the president of the company called me and asked if would consider returning as Vice President of Sales, if I could work from home. And that's what I have been doing. I go to the home office 3 days out of the month and everyone is happy. And this all happened after a very "rich friend" of mine took the time and prayed for me from his car on the way to a show in NY.

Rich Friends are a treasure

Ron

From: Julian Phillips [mailto:julesmp1@msn.com]

I'm overwhelmed. God is good, isn't He?!
Have a blessed day Ron, and may His goodness and mercy continue to follow you and your family ALL the days of your life.

10
"STANDING AT THE GATE"

Barbara works for a social service agency in Harlem called The Northside Center for Child Development. For a few years they have produced a food drive for needy residents around the holidays and it's usually a big deal. Paula White Ministries sponsored at least two of these events, and they have provided boxes filled with non-perishable foods and house-hold items. Needless to say, hundreds of families participate and of course that means Northside usually reaches out for volunteers to help in this monumental effort to provide boxes for everyone who has need.

A few years ago I decided to become a volunteer and help out. It was right after the New Year and I had nothing of importance on my plate. Besides all of that I really wanted to be with Barbara and do something constructive on a cold Saturday morning.

Paula White Ministries had a huge eighteen wheeler chock full of boxes that were filled to capacity with all sorts of goodies. Carefully placed in neat rows, volunteers were at the ready to help distribute the goods to crowds of people waiting on the streets outside of the gated building that was used for distribution. I decided that I would position myself with some volunteers who were handing out cups of hot apple cider to the crowd eagerly waiting to pick up boxes. The hot apple cider stand was strategically placed at the front gate. Before those gates were opened, I decided to take a look to see just how many people were on line. It must have been at least three city blocks of people waiting for those gates to open! Sipping on some cider I too was waiting for the gate to open. It was getting cold and knew we would be in for a long day.

Now maybe I looked the part that day, dressed in a long dark coat and a small brimmed fedora, but I've heard this before. "Are you a preacher"? , a man at the very front of the line asked me as soon as the gate opened.

"Yes", I said somewhat reluctantly. As I mentioned, I have been asked this so many times. This time just out of sheer frustration, I decided to give in and just go with the flow. I certainly did not want to misrepresent God, but I have had at least three people over the span of thirty years – two ministers, and one Pentecostal woman who worked for the National Council of Churches, tell me about this 'Calling' I had on my life.

"Would you pray for me?", he asked. I could smell the liquor on his breath, but I could also see the desperation in his eyes. "Sure", I said. As he came through the gate and up the steps, I laid hands on his head. Immediately he fell to his knees and began to cry. That reaction as I laid hands on this man startled me, but I kept focus and continued to pray over this man. As if on cue, other people asked for prayer. One of our church friends who also came to volunteer that morning started to bring people over to me.

"I can feel the power flowing from you!" exclaimed this Hispanic woman who started crying as I prayed and embraced her. God's power flowing from me? She had to be completely out of her mind, I thought, but I could not ignore the effect my prayer had on her.

Prayer broke out all over the courtyard inside the gate that morning and afternoon. People gathered in small groups to pray. I even had a woman pray for me! It was simply a wonderful spectacle. Folks who need food also got another gift. I must say God showed up in a big way that morning. It all started with an unsuspecting person, (me), standing at the gate, who was just there to help volunteer and hand out apple cider.

11

"FLIGHT TO NEW ORLEANS"

After 15 terms in office, Congressman Edolphus Towns decided he had enough and threw in the towel. Towns was a senior member of Congress and served as Chairman of the powerful Government Oversight and Reform Committee. I must say after working with him as Communications Director for two years I was somewhat relieved – even though I had no job to transition into at the time. Politics is a rough business and not an easy place to survive. Any day on Capitol Hill or even in the District can be a dogfight, with no permanent friends or enemies. While I was extremely grateful the Congressman had saved Barbara and me from certain foreclosure two years earlier, I knew after just my first day, the world of politics was not for me! The question became very simple. What next?!

Now that I was free to put my hat back in the ring in the world of news, I wasted no time contacting my agent to send out demo reels to the networks. Perhaps now with two years in the political area, I might be a more valuable asset to news executives. At the same time, I also considered my other passion, and that was cooking. Back in 2005, I won a national celebrity recipe contest over the likes of Chef Emeril, among others. It was grilled salmon smothered with black bean sauce. A simple recipe, but I think I won the hearts of those who read the column 'Fave Foods of the Famous' in newspapers and online, because it was tasty –

and more importantly, very easy to prepare. Excited over the honor, I cooked the dish 'live' on Fox & Friends one Saturday morning.

Cooking was something in my blood from a young child. When I became a news personality, I always brought something into the stations where I worked for the staff. Ribs, chicken, you name it, I would rustle up something for folks to eat. For me, there is simply no better feeling seeing the smile on the faces of people eating your food!

"You should name your restaurant The Sound Bite" said Kenny Hogan, one of my cameramen at Channel 11, one day while we were sitting in a crew car after finishing an assignment. "With all of your years in the news biz, there must be a connection to your past." Kenny uttered those words fifteen years before I actually incorporated the name. I had the idea of opening up a food establishment way back then. Once the name was incorporated shortly after leaving the Congressman's office, I ran into Kenny on the street one day and recounted the story. He did not remember, but that in itself is another story!

Filing for unemployment was not something I was looking forward to, but it was money, nonetheless. All the while, my mind was clearly focused on this restaurant venture, even more so than landing another news gig. How would I start? How would I raise the money? Who could I find to partner with me? Cooking was one thing, running and managing a restaurant was an entirely different matter. Was I biting off more than I could chew this time? I sorely needed a Word from God to make sure this was the right thing to do. Of course after much prayer, I was not getting anything, or at least that is what I thought!

About six months before I left the Congressman's office, I was experimenting in the kitchen one afternoon trying to come up with something different to do with chicken wings. I was a huge fan of Chef Paul Prudhomme, who invented the technique of blackening fish and meats. I never really knew anyone who was blackening chicken wings. Everything about wings is frying, grilling or baking. Why not blackened wings? Well, I took an old cast iron skillet and got some Cajun seasonings and went to town! After about 30 taste tests from New York to North Carolina, I was hooked – and so was everyone else who tasted them! This was the move. "I'm going to revolutionize the wing industry with these blackened wings!", I said to myself. After doing much research I realized part of the answer was right in front of me. It was Paul Prudhomme. He had a spice factory in New Orleans and they made custom spices for restaurants!

About a week after leaving the Congressman's office and really wanting to move forward with the restaurant venture, I needed to get down to Prudhomme's factory and meet with his executives. Simple enough except for one huge obstacle – we had no money! How could I get there? Time was certainly a factor, but I had no clue how to pull this off.

Another week had passed and still no idea on how I was going to make my way to New Orleans. "You guys got time for dinner tonight?" Linda North said to Barbara over the phone. Linda was a songwriter Barbara had worked with. Her husband, John, ran a successful business. They are a nice couple and have turned out to be good friends over the years. Dinner with Linda and John is always an experience so we were both looking forward to it.

"What are you up to these days Julian?", John asked over a glass of post dinner wine. "I'm looking to open a restaurant. The thing is I need to get to New Orleans and meet with Paul Prudhomme's staff to make some custom spices." Linda and John knew our financial situation, so I really did not have to explain I didn't have the funds to travel to New Orleans.

"When do you need to go Julian?" asked John with this inquisitive look on his face. "Well, the sooner the better" I exclaimed. "I just so happen to be flying down to New Orleans to attend a food convention in two weeks. Do you and Barbara want to come?" Now John knew I did not have the money. Why would he even ask? What I did not know came as a total surprise, and a tremendous blessing from the next thing that came out of his mouth.

"I have my own plane. You and Barbara can fly down with me". Stunned at hearing the news, I looked over at Barbara across the table, who was also speechless. After a few seconds of silence, which seemed like an eternity I said, "How much will this cost?" "Nothing at all, just make me a few sandwiches for the trip there and back".

Out of nowhere, or so it seemed, we were on our way to New Orleans. I knew where this blessing came from – and perhaps just as importantly, I also knew I was on the right path.

12
"PSALM 138"

The holidays were always good times for me when I hosted the Weekend Fox & Friends show. Good in a sense that I would usually get positive emails from viewers. During the course of the year, I would have some fans, however since I was not as conservative as the majority of our viewers, I would get a lot of e-mails let's say that bordered on downright hate! It was not the most pleasant of experiences, but it comes with the territory. When you sign on to become a personality on the big or small screen, you will be open to all sorts of scrutiny from the public. It doesn't matter if you're a news anchor, athlete, entertainer, or whatever. If you don't have the stomach for criticism whether it's fair or just plain off the wall, find another profession. There is also another life changer being in the spotlight. You simply can't go to the same places, or do the same things you used to do in public when you were an ordinary citizen. There are certain places, no matter how innocent they may seem, that are off limits when you are considered a 'celebrity' – at least if you want to maintain a certain image of respectability . You are always 'on stage' when you are in public.

After about a year of sifting through all the negative mail, I just stopped looking at it. It was not helpful to my mission of trying to provide different perspectives on national and world affairs for an audience not really willing to consider points of view other than their own, but I pressed on.

"This is not the first e-mail we've gotten like this. Be careful". A not so flattering e-mail blasting my political views had reached the front office. Kevin Magee, Vice president of Programming, who was my boss, shared the email with me. He was a great person to work for and I believe was just looking out for my best interests. Nevertheless, it was not what I wanted to see or hear from him when I was just trying to do my job.

A few weeks had passed since I got that email from Magee, and needless to say even the strongest person can get sidetracked after enough abuse. I was a little depressed to say the least. Couldn't people 'agree to disagree' without being so hateful? It seemed like the world of cable news created this tension between the 'left' and the 'right'. I remember the days when Tip O'Neil, the Speaker of the House would publicly disagree with President Reagan's policies – but at the end of the day, it would not be uncommon to see the two of them discussing things over a glass of scotch in the Oval Office. Congressman Towns used to talk about the days when House Republicans and Democrats challenged each other in basketball games around the country. Having a different opinion did not mean you were any less American. Sadly, the country has changed.

I was invited to be a part of a news panel discussing current political events at the New York Sheraton Hotel. I must admit I was getting a little battle weary and was not much up for a political dogfight, but I agreed to go. After the panel discussion, two men approached me. "We just want you to know that we are two right wing Hawks from Colorado and we don't agree with much you have to say on Fox News" said one of the gentleman. "However we really like listening to you because you force us to think and examine our beliefs". I was shocked! This was the very reason I got into journalism. I walked out of the Sheraton with a new sense of purpose.

As I mentioned opening up this chapter, the holidays were always good times for me on Fox because I was allowed to read scripture on the air during Christmas and Easter. The folks in the Bible Belt always loved me when I did this. I guess it was some sort of truce between two opposing forces. "I know Christmas is supposed to be a time of cheer and joy, but there are many people who get depressed during the holidays.

I would like to read verses 7-8 from Chapter 138 in the book of Psalms and I hope this will lift your spirits".

"Though I walk in the midst of trouble, you preserve my life; you stretch out your hand against the anger of my foes, with your right hand you save me. The lord will fulfill His purpose for me; your love, O Lord, endures forever – do not abandon the works of your hands" (NIV)

It was a Sunday morning and I rushed off the news set to head to church. As soon as I entered the green room, one of the production assistants handed me an e-mail. "I think you will want to read this e-mail", she said with a smile on her face. It was from a viewer in Michigan.

"Julian I don't always agree with what you have to say, but I was about to do something very desperate before you read that Psalm. Thank you very much."

I stood there gazing at that letter for several minutes before I left for church. I showed it to my pastor who smiled after reading it. If God's only reason sending me to Fox was to save just one life, I figure enduring all that hate mail was worth it.

13

"Unmerited Favor"

Being young and foolish is one thing, but being a little older and remaining foolish is quite another!

I had just completed a round of golf at The Links at Shirley, an upscale public course in Shirley, Long Island. Satisfied with a pretty good round, I packed up my clubs and put them in my 1994 Mazda R-X7. If you know anything about cars, the R-X7 is a classic roadster. Two hundred fifty-five horse power with a sequential twin turbo rotary engine under the hood! This two seater remains one of the best handling sports cars ever made – not to mention a top speed of about one hundred fifty miles per hour on a stock production model. I must admit I could not resist the temptation to take on those foolish enough to challenge me in head-to-head drag races on the open highways in the wee hours of the morning. But as I mentioned, I was young and foolish.

Punching through the gears, I'd just entered the Long island Expressway at exit 68, getting ready for the 45 minute or so ride back to Port Washington. Seemingly out of nowhere an Audi pulled up on one side and a Porsche on the other. We all looked at each other and the testosterone began acting up! The next thing you know I'm sandwiched in between two cars reaching a speed of about eighty miles per hour. Well with all the excitement I did not see what the two cars to my left and right saw. The Suffolk County Highway Patrol! They slowed down in time, and I barreled ahead. "License and registration please" said the officer. "Did you know how fast you were going"? "About 75?" I said, knowing it was a lie. "I clocked you at 83 miles per hour". Well one lie lead to another. "I just finished a round of golf and I was rushing home to take my wife out for her birthday". I then proceeded to engage him in a conversation about golf and he obliged. "I'm going back to my car and I'll be back shortly", the officer said with a smile. I figured I sweet talked my way out of a ticket.

"He's your ticket sir". "I'm really sorry for speeding officer, would these PBA cards help me out of this ticket?" "Sorry sir, those cards don't give you the right to speed". He was right. I was so wrong, but I had a clean driving record and did not want any blemishes on it.

"What can I do about this Pastor? I have a clean record and Suffolk County does not have a plea bargain. Either you are guilty or innocent. No excuses!" "Just ask God for mercy and see what happens", is all he could say. What else could he say? I was dead wrong and was not willing to pay the price.

When it came to filling out the part regarding guilty or innocent, I lied again and filled out innocent. Expecting God's mercy on a lie was not really something I expected, but I foolishly lied anyway and figured I'd take my chances in a court of law.

A month had passed and it was my time to head to the Suffolk County Traffic Court. I was praying that the officer who issued the ticket would not show up. It was my only chance of getting the ticket thrown out. It was not unusual for officers not to show up, but of course as I entered the courtroom, there he was! I smiled and tried to make conversation, but he did not remember me. He was there to testify before the judge with numerous tickets he had written on that day. With each and every case, the officer uttered the orchestrated response in saying how his radar device is scientifically calibrated and could not possibly be wrong in detecting speeds.

"Guilty!" yelled the judge to everyone who stood before him! He was tough, no doubt, and after each and every case before mine, I became certain I was doomed to pay a fine and get a point or two on my license. I had lied anyway, so at this point how could I possibly expect God to bail me out – and better yet, why?

My time to stand before this judge was at hand. The officer stood next to me and as with custom, the case number was read and the judge explained to the court why I was there, then proceeded to ask the officer his version of events. Just as in all the cases before mine, the officer went into his usual song and dance about his device and how he correctly clocked me at eighty three miles per hour. "Just finish your point", I said to myself so I could give my version ad then take my punishment.

Suddenly after about thirty seconds into his testimony, the officer fell sick and asked the judge if he could leave the courtroom! The judge granted his request and as the officer left, the judge turned to me and said "I'm going to give the officer ten minutes to compose himself and resume this case sir". Clearly the judge was itching to fine and give me a penalty. "Ok, your honor", I said and calmly went back to take a seat in the courtroom.

About ten minutes later, the officer came back into the courtroom and the judge called us both back to the bench. "Are you ready to resume your testimony?", the judge asked the officer. "Yes your honor!" In the strangest thing I have ever seen, the officer fell sick again within seconds of trying to finish his testimony. "I can't finish this your honor. Do with him what you will", as he staggered out of the courtroom. A silence fell over those in the courtroom. Some people looked on in disbelief!

"I just want you to know Mr. Phillips that I would have found you guilty, but since the officer could not finish his testimony, I have no choice but to dismiss this case". With that, I thanked the judge and walked out of the courtroom to the bathroom before heading home. As I entered the bathroom, the officer emerged from one of the stalls. "I don't know what happened to me in there, but I'm glad you got off. You seem like a nice guy". What could I say at this point? I was just as stunned as everyone else. "Thank you officer", I said. "I hope you are okay".

With that, I dashed out of the bathroom and down to the lobby to call Barbara before heading home, to tell her about the bizarre series of events. As I got off the phone, there was a man who was in the courtroom and he approached me. "I've never seen anything like that before", he said. "I'm a Christian!", I proudly proclaimed. "So am I", he said as he walked off.

There is no way I deserved favor in this case. I lied – multiple times – but yet, in one of the strangest events I can recall in my life. I received favor. I have no moral to the ending of this story other than that God works in mysterious ways. Needless to say, I felt kind of guilty for His grace, but I was extremely grateful for His unmerited favor.

14

"Saved By Grace"

Agolf-a-holic will travel almost anywhere and do almost anything to play a round of golf. Make no mistake about it, I'm a golf-a-holic and proud of it! I love the game and even started a Golf Ministry at the Christian Cultural Center. Golf ministry? Actually, yes. There are a lot of parallels between the game of golf and the Christian walk of faith. So many, that numerous books have been written about it, but that is a story for another time.

It was an early Saturday morning and the trip to the Cherry Creek Golf Course would take a little over an hour. The distance to Riverhead, Long Island from my house in Port Washington was about fifty miles and I had an early tee time. I packed up my clubs and put them in the passenger seat of my R-X7 and rushed out of the house at about 6 a.m. to insure I would get to the course on time. There are about a million golf courses much closer to my house, but I wanted to play Cherry Creek. It's a nice public course with a grass driving range. There are very few public courses with grass driving ranges. There's something about hitting those practice balls on real grass as opposed to rubber mats that makes all the difference in preparing for a round! Outside of that, I love walking on to a driving range early in the morning with not many other golfers around. I can hit and take in nature at the same time. It's a beautiful thing to get lost in your thoughts, while trying to straighten out the kinks in your swing when the sun has just appeared over the horizon.

About ten miles into the trek to Riverhead, I noticed a loud noise coming from the front of my car. At first, I paid it no attention, but then about halfway to Riverhead I could feel the car pulling to the right. Anyone with some sense would have gotten off the highway to look for a service station. Not me! Mr. Knucklehead decides to continue on to the course!

As I said, I'm a golf-a-holic. Nothing, I mean nothing, was going to get in the way of an early tee time at Cherry Creek!

For some reason God looks out for children and fools. I happen to fall into both categories. I made it to the course, however as I pulled into a parking space, the noise got much louder as I turned the steering wheel and I could feel something was terribly wrong. Nonetheless, I figured I'd deal with the car after the round of golf. I was focused on getting my 'game' on!

About three hours later, and a mediocre game, I packed up the clubs and put them in the car. At this point, my focus was on that noise and the steering problems. I'm fifty miles from home and don't have a clue about any mechanics on the east end of Long island. To make matters worse, there are not many mechanics who have the knowledge to work on RX-7's in the first place. On top of that, I knew of no Mazda dealerships in Riverhead. I sat there for a moment and then prayed that the car would hold up till I made it back to Port Washington.

I cranked it up and headed out of the parking lot onto the country road heading back into Riverhead. As I continued on this two lane road, the steering was really starting to malfunction. I could only pray—and I did once again that it would hold up until I got back home.

As I reached the main road in Riverhead that leads to the main highway I just happened to look to my right and saw a Mazda dealership! I was just about to pass it, but *something* persuaded me to pull in.

"Can I help you sir?" a service representative said as I got out of the car. "Actually yes. I'm having a problem with my steering and I have a long ride back west. I need someone to take a look and tell me what may be the problem." "Well come on in and take a seat in the service area. I'll have someone take down your information in just a few minutes", he said with a smile. Somehow I knew this was not going to be a cheap visit to the repair shop. This was going to be an expensive round of golf, but at least my mind was at ease in the fact I just *happened* to come across a Mazda dealership before I hit the highway.

"Julian, is that you?!" Standing in front of me was Jim Kincaid, the service manager for the Mazda dealership in Hempstead, Long Island where I purchased my car a few years back. He was a nice guy and I was sad he left that dealership because we developed a bond and I knew I could count on him and his staff to properly take care of my RX-7. It was my baby and good mechanics are extremely hard to come by.

"Man are you a sight for sore eyes!" I said after a brief embrace. "How long you been out here?" "Oh just a few months. I bounced around a bit and landed up here in Riverhead. What's the problem with the RX-7?" Jim asked. "Well I started hearing this noise in the front end and then my steering started to go. Don't know what's wrong but you know it's a long ride back. Stumbling upon this dealership and running into you. Talk about luck!"

"Have a seat. We just so happen to have one of the best RX-7 mechanics on Long Island. We'll get back to you shortly after taking a look at things".

After about 20 minutes or so, Jim came back with this look of concern on his face. "Somebody much be watching out for you my friend". You had two bolts missing that connect the struts on the driver's side. If you got on the highway and hit just one bump going more than fifty miles per hour on the way back home – well let's just say you could have been seriously injured, or even worse!"

After the repair was made, I thanked Jim and hopped in the car for the ride home. Imagine the timing. It was perfect! Everything lined up to prevent me from getting on that highway with my beloved RX-7 in that condition. Was it coincidence? Some skeptic might find a way to explain it all away, but I *knew* without a doubt, I was saved by His grace.

15
"PURPOSE"

Sometimes things that happen to you in life that just can't be reasoned. An extraordinary event or circumstance that when you try to explain it – or better yet get somebody to believe it, they most certainly will insist you are not telling the truth or just may be exaggerating more than a little bit. Such was the case for me when I was a kid growing up in St. Albans, Queens New York.

I don't really remember the year or my exact age, but I was in the basement of a friend's house. There were several of us gathered there hanging out and having fun.

There was this dart board nailed to the wall of the basement. Playing darts was popular back then and we were all throwing these steel darts with the plastic feathers towards this dart board trying to hit the bulls-eye.

There was this kid, I can't remember his name either, who was fascinated with the darts. He later turned out to be an accomplished martial artist as an adult. But that afternoon, after everyone else was finished playing with the dart board, this kid kept on throwing at the board. Quite some time had passed and as I said, we all moved on to other games. With the dart board a distant memory for us, or so I thought, I

47

decided to sit down in a chair directly under the board, not realizing it was still being used as a target by this kid.

The next thing I know is that I saw him wind up and throw. Perhaps he didn't realize how close the dart board was to me directly overhead, or maybe he thought he was that good. Whatever the case, this steel dart comes flying out of his hand, and not at the dart board overhead, but directly at me!

As I mentioned earlier, some things you just can't explain. I did not have time to duck, because it happened so fast, but as the dart was inches from my forehead it somehow changed direction and flew past the left side of my face, finding a place in the wooden wall!

The kid was stunned realizing he could have seriously injured me. No more darts were thrown by him or anyone else that afternoon. I have no idea how that dart could have made what seemed to be a ninety degree angle turn right in front of my face.

As a kid, I went to Sunday school and knew about Jesus, but what did I know about things like purpose? Not much. Pastor Bernard always talks about purpose. Pastor Rick Warren wrote a book called "The Purpose "Driven Life", which has sold millions of copies world-wide. Reflecting back on things as an adult, I reckoned that God spared me from serious injury or death for a reason that afternoon. I mean a dart doesn't just change course like that!

Purpose is a funny thing. Pastor Bernard says, we as human beings need a purpose in life, something to live for. The good news is, no matter our lot in life, God does have a purpose for each and every one of us. The thing is, God does not tell us our purpose – we must discover it! I'm still on the road to discovery.

16

"A Prayer Answered"

Watching someone struggle through a life threatening illness is tough. It's even worse when it happens to be a loved one or a family member. My father was diagnosed with cancer in 1986. He started to lose a lot of weight and I could tell he was concerned because he was a big man and he did not change his diet in any way. I guess it must have been a little fear mixed in with desperation, because he started to load up on candy and sweets to gain weight.

The following months, we all watched him transform into a shell of his former self. Bedridden and in much pain, he did not complain much. In fact, he fought cancer much like he fought every other challenge in his life – with courage. Years of fighting the federal government over discrimination, personal disappointments and being part of a generation of African Americans that fell victim to Jim Crow and racial segregation, left him bitter at times. Nevertheless in his dying days, he said "I had a good life".

Kids seldom understand the things adults go through and for a long time I did not like my father much because the pain he went through often found its' way to my mother, my sister and me. As an adult, I finally understood the root causes of a lot of the pain he went through and it was not until then that I could forgive him. Cecil Phillips left this world in 1987, the fighter he always was in life. He went down swinging. I gotta give it to him, he fought a good fight.

The day after the funeral, Barbara and I went to play paddle ball in a park on Washington Avenue in Brooklyn about a block or so from our apartment. For some time we dreamed about owning a brownstone, but they were far too expensive for us in the Clinton Hill section. Lord knows we spent a lot of time looking. Well right after that funeral we both prayed again for God to find us a house. After the loss of our father we needed something to help relieve the pain.

Just after we finished playing a number of games and were headed back home, as we turned around, there was this brownstone across the street from the park with a for 'sale sign' in the window. Curious, we both walked across the street and took down the number. The brownstone was being completely renovated. Surely we would not be able to afford it, but we called anyway. To our surprise, the price was just right! We purchased the brownstone and lived there for a number of years before moving to Long Island. It was truly a prayer answered. Yet another example of *empirical evidence*. God became real to us when we needed evidence of His existence. Not in a book, not from someone else's experience, but His reality in our lives.

Empirical evidence. Is God real to *you*? Examine your life and see where and when He 'showed up'. If you don't think He has, *ask* Him to. He surely will!